Toward a Co Framework for the Study of Folklore and the Internet

Trevor J. Blank

A **Current Arguments in Folklore** selection from *Folklore and the Internet: Vernacular Expression in a Digital World* with new material

Toward a Conceptual Framework for the Study of Folklore and the Internet comprises chapter 1 from *Folklore and the Internet: Vernacular Expression in a Digital World* by Trevor J. Blank © 2009 by University Press of Colorado, and new material by Trevor J. Blank © 2014 by University Press of Colorado.

Published by Utah State University Press
An imprint of University Press of Colorado
5589 Arapahoe Avenue, Suite 206C
Boulder, Colorado 80303

The University Press of Colorado is a proud member of The Association of American University Presses.

The University Press of Colorado is a cooperative publishing enterprise supported, in part, by Adams State University, Colorado State University, Fort Lewis College, Metropolitan State University of Denver, Regis University, University of Colorado, University of Northern Colorado, Utah State University, and Western State Colorado University.

Library of Congress Cataloging-in-Publication Data for the book *Folklore and the Internet: Vernacular Expression in a Digital World*
Folklore and the internet: vernacular expression in a digital world / edited by Trevor J. Blank.
p. cm.
Includes bibliographical references and index.
ISBN 978-0-87421-750-6 (pbk.: alk. paper) — ISBN 978-0-87421-751-3 (e-book)
1. Folklore and the Internet. 2. Folklore—Computer network resources. 3. Digital
communications. I. Blank, Trevor J.
GR44.E43F65 2009
                    398.02854678—dc22
                    2009026813

USU Press Current Arguments in Folklore edition, 2014
eISBN 978-0-87421-945-6

DOI: 10.7330_9780874219456.c001

Contents

Current Arguments in Folklore

Toward a Conceptual Framework for the Study of Folklore and the Internet

THE CHALLENGES AND PROMISE OF FOLKLORE IN THE DIGITAL AGE

ONE AFTERNOON AT THE 2009 ANNUAL MEETING of the American Folklore Society in Boise, Idaho—just one month after the release of *Folklore and the Internet*—I went out to lunch with a small group of folklorists. Catching up over an impressive array of potatoes and other local fare, we eventually began to discuss our new and ongoing research endeavors of late. When it was my turn to speak, I excitedly announced that I had been studying Internet folklore, and that I was conducting some ethnographic fieldwork online.[1] Before I could break into another sentence I was cut off by a veteran folklorist among us who scoffed, "You can't *do* fieldwork on the Internet." Leaning forward with a dismissive grin, the scholar asserted: "To do fieldwork, you must first have a *field* to work in," concluding, "There is no such thing as true ethnography online."[2] I wasn't hurt or surprised by the remarks; I had heard them before.[3] Nevertheless, I present this anecdote because it encapsulates the tenor of skepticism regarding folkloristic scholarship on Internet and burgeoning new media

DOI: 10.7330_9780874219456.c001

technologies that epitomized the time.[4] But that was 2009. And fortunately, a lot has changed over the last five years.

When *Folklore and the Internet* was released on September 9, 2009, it became the first edited volume dedicated specifically to the folkloristic analysis of emergent digital technologies.[5] Accordingly, my introduction to the anthology, "Toward a Conceptual Framework for the Study of Folklore and the Internet," aimed to bring folklorists up to speed on existing scholarly literature and arguments while working to establish the Internet as a legitimate area for folkloristic inquiry. In an era where some incredulous folklorists were perhaps more inclined to side with the scholar who chided my interests in digital ethnography, the book and its introductory framework managed to break through, and they have held up over time. Indeed, the publication of this very monograph underscores the positive impact those bodies of writing have enjoyed within folklore studies.

In November 2012, *Folklore and the Internet* was followed by another edited volume, *Folk Culture in the Digital Age* (Blank 2012a), which built upon the success of its predecessor to boast a more theoretically expansive analysis of folklore and new media technology. The anthology's introduction further documented the indisputable encroachment of digital traditions in the corporeal world (and vice versa[6]) while also highlighting emergent patterns of vernacular expression and discourse proliferating via technologically mediated communication (Blank 2012b). Most importantly, the introduction to *Folk Culture in the Digital Age* endeavored to recalibrate parts of the conceptual framework and underlying argumentation proposed in *Folklore and the Internet* to better account for the new contexts, constraints, and expressive modes that had surfaced in the three short years since its publication.[7] This designedly included stepping back from earlier emphases on issues of privacy and anonymity in online settings; the merits of conducting cyberethnographic fieldwork; and complaints about the disciplinary boundaries of folkloristics—themes represented heavily in *Folklore and the Internet*'s introduction—because those areas of concern and resistance had substantially waned or been abandoned altogether. Moreover, new sources of discontent took their place. Herein lies the great challenge of collecting and analyzing contemporary folklore.

As digital folklore evolves, so too do the expressive repertoires of its purveyors, thus necessitating a reexamination of how folklorists actively interpret the domain. Time passes quicker than ever in the digital age; praxis[8] amalgamates as newfangled discursive practices and expressive genres are vernacularly established in rapid-fire succession. And so the recurring cycle of updating and reappropriating the folklorist's mission and purview for studying the Internet is largely a response to the breakneck speed in which digital technologies advance and are then notably adopted by the folk. To be sure, the need for constant revision or expansion of the theories, scope, and approaches that inform the study of folklore and the Internet presents both a blessing and a curse. The perpetual, exponential growth of Internet and new media technologies leave hybridized folklore and folk culture in a constant, exhausting state of flux. Furthermore, the amount of time between the completion of a scholar's initial research and analytical write-up and the work's subsequent journey through the peer review, editing, and publication process is often lamentably considerable.[9] As a result, it is exceedingly difficult to produce representatively current folklore research when the pace of digital culture so effortlessly eclipses the rate in which such material reaches print; by the time a new folkloristic essay finally arrives, its sources and arguments may already be antiquated and in need of corrective emendation.[10] But these are minor inconveniences to surmount. Administrative hurdles notwithstanding, there is a great deal more to be excited about when it comes to the trajectories of folklore and folkloristics in the digital age.[11]

The utilization of cellphones, smartphones, tablets, laptops, desktop computers, and other Internet-capable devices for vernacular expression, social networking, and general correspondence exemplifies the remarkable power and reach of technologically mediated communication.[12] Individuals can meaningfully engage in an intricate web of symbolic interaction that offers a performative venue for sharing "creepypasta" narratives,[13] curating one's own social media profile or identity (Aldred 2010; Baym 2010; Dobler 2009; McNeill 2009, 84), generating or forwarding memes (Blank 2012b, 8–11; Foote 2007; Kaplan 2013, 136–39; McNeill 2009; 2013, 179–84), and humorously Photoshopping images in order to tacitly comment on current events, emic contexts, or elements of popular culture.[14] Collaboration and group activity is a mainstay of the digital realm (Shirky 2008; see also McNeill 2012). Niche communities, forums, and fan sites abound (Ellis 2012; Howard 2011; see also Chayko 2008; Rheingold 2000), as do wikis, which rely on users' perennial cooperation to form and regulate a particular digital space (see Westerman 2009).[15] And the ubiquitous use of digital technologies for expressive communication has led to the hybridization of folk culture, interchangeably drawing from corporeal and virtual traditions in the creation of new folklore.[16] These subjects have steadily accrued greater attention in folkloristic scholarship since the 2009 debut of *Folklore and the Internet*, but there is still work to be done.

It is easy to take for granted how freely information can now be accessed, but the consequential impact on the transmission of folk knowledge is unmistakable. Technologically mediated communication presents a seemingly endless, regenerating corpus of expressive content ripe for folkloristic analysis.[17] Folklorists must continue to meticulously chronicle how the shifting tides of technology influence and shape vernacular discourse. However, this task may regularly require a reconsideration of existing methods and conceptual frameworks given the ever-changing digital landscape and the multifaceted folklore it serves to create, extinguish, adopt, modify, cultivate, and disseminate. After all, as communication theorist Marshall McLuhan noted in 1955: "It is the framework which changes with each new technology and not just the picture within the frame" (McLuhan and Zingrone 1996, 273).

BUILDING THE FRAMEWORK

In his essay "Toward a Definition of Folklore in Context," Dan Ben-Amos asserts: "If the initial assumption of folklore research is based on the disappearance of its subject matter, there is no way to prevent the science from following the same road" (Ben-Amos 1971, 14). In similar fashion, Alan Dundes began his presidential plenary address to the American Folklore Society in 2004 with a grim outlook on the future of the discipline by contending that the "state of folkloristics at the beginning of the twenty-first century is depressingly worrisome" (Dundes 2005, 385). Such alarm-sounding statements merit our attention, but the fact remains that this has been a recurring assertion within this academic discipline for some time (Oring 1998). Richard Dorson lamented in 1972 that in "a few more years, there will be no more folklore, and *ergo*, no need for any folklorists" (Dorson 1972, 41); but as Dorson "responded by looking elsewhere and [subsequently] found folklore in the media and a folk in the city" (Kirshenblatt-Gimblett 1998, 302), we too must respond by looking elsewhere when such feelings of impending doom surface in folklore scholarship.

Folklore is a self-conscious discipline, and speculation on the future of folkloristics—the academic study of folklore—has been pessimistic at best. In a similar vein, Richard Bauman and Charles L. Briggs note that tradition "has been reportedly on the verge of dying for more than three centuries, [yet] . . . continues to provide useful means of producing and legitimizing new modernist projects, sets of legislators, and schemes of social inequality" (Bauman and Briggs 2003, 306). Despite all of the doom and gloom, folklore "continues to be alive and well in the modern world, due in part to increased transmission via e-mail and the Internet" (Dundes 2005, 406). It is time that folklorists look to the Internet, not only to expand our scholastic horizons but also to carry our discipline into the digital age.

The formulation of the World Wide Web network has its roots in the Cold War tensions of the mid-twentieth century. The earliest incarnations were spawned in the form of the US Department of Defense's Advanced Research Projects Agency Network (ARPANET), created mainly in response to the Soviet Union's launching of Sputnik. Beginning in 1958, ARPANET served the military and academic researchers as a means of communication and as a command tool for defense operations. E-mail technology was created in 1970, and by the 1980s people were interacting online through bulletin boards (discussion groups), MUDs (multiuser dungeons), and the WELL (Whole Earth 'Lectronic Link), a social network composed of Internet users from across the globe; later, Internet Relay Chat (IRC) followed (Hafner and Lyon 1998).[18]

The modern Internet emerged with the creation of the World Wide Web in 1989 by English computer scientist Timothy Berners-Lee. The development of HyperText Markup Language (HTML) and web browser technology allowed the Internet to expand from an exclusive academic forum into the worldwide phenomenon it is today. In 1992, the Internet was opened to the public domain.

At the beginning of the 1990s there took place a fundamental transformation of the Internet . . . as the web became the center of the Internet and web browsers became the most common way of accessing it, transformations in the communication processes established over the Internet also took place due to the specific characteristic of the web and its browsers. The web introduced new ways of communicating over the Internet, facilitated the use of the net, leading to its popularization, and, to a great extent, also facilitated and promoted its commercialization (Bermejo 2007, 73).

As the Internet developed as a communications facilitator, folklore emerged as recognizably on it as it did in "the real world." From the earliest moments of the modern Internet's existence, folklore was a central component of the domain, moderating the intersection of computer professionals with hackers, newfangled lingo, and the dispersal of stories, pranks, and legends (Jennings 1990).[19] Bruce McClelland notes that as a result, "the boundary between the actual and the virtual began to become blurred" (McClelland 2000, 182). Established academics recognized both the power presented by the burgeoning of Internet folklore and the importance carried by studying it: "Right now, all we have on the Net is folklore, like the Netiquette that old-timers try to teach the flood of new arrivals, and debates about freedom of expression versus nurturance of community . . . A science of Net behavior is not going to reshape the way people behave on-line, but knowledge of the dynamics of how people do behave is an important social feedback loop to install if the Net is to be self-governing at any scale" (Rheingold 2000, 64).[20] But while folklore emerged on the Internet, folklorists generally did not follow it.

When the World Wide Web took off in the 1990s, the allied disciplines of anthropology, sociology, and communication studies began paying careful attention to various sociocultural dimensions of the Internet, but amid this dialogue only a small handful of thoughtful folkloristic articles on the burgeoning Internet culture appeared (Baym 1993; Dorst 1990; Howard 1997; Kirshenblatt-Gimblett 1995, 1996; Roush 1997). With few exceptions, folklorists have generally neglected the Internet as a venue for academic inquiry for nearly two decades, and a large portion of the existing literature on folklore and the Internet has been penned by armchair folklorists—scholars untrained in the vocabulary and methodologies of the discipline—through the lens of social science, communication, and literature degrees. Each year, the American Folklore Society's annual meeting boasts more papers and panels on folklore and the Internet than the year before, yet these papers have not found their way to a culminating publication. One of the first and only specialized folkloristic examinations of the Internet took place on the electronic pages of the graduate-student-run *Folklore Forum* of Indiana University,[21] which published a special issue on the topic in spring 2007 (volume 37, no. 1); the issue featured only *two* original articles on the topic (Blank 2007; Foote 2007).[22]

To seek out folkloristic literature about the Internet is to spend numerous hours piecing together data strewn about aimlessly, spanning many years and multiple publications. *Folklore Forum* notwithstanding, no comprehensive work that details the folkloristic approach to the study of the Internet has been produced to date. It is my hope that this book will help to fill that void. In a discipline seemingly obsessed with a fear of its own demise, the Internet provides a limitless frontier for contemporary scholastic possibilities. If it is currency we seek, then we needn't look further. "It is here, in the heat of a nascent technology," writes Kirshenblatt-Gimblett, "that we can contemplate what folklore's contemporary subject might be," adding that "electronic communication offers an opportunity to rethink folklore's disciplinary givens and to envision a fully contemporary subject. It is not a matter of finding folklore analogues between the paperless office and the paperwork empire. The differences are consequential" (Kirshenblatt-Gimblett 1995, 72–73).

So why have folklorists taken so long to systematically study the impact of the Internet? The exact reasons that folklorists as a group have predominantly ignored the Internet and technologically based folklore are uncertain. Folklore theory holds that folkloric expression is reflective and serves as a "mirror" of societal and cultural values; folklorists should therefore use this mirror to analyze society and culture. This ought to encourage a scholarly examination of the Internet, due to this format's status as a major agent of communication (especially over the last decade). Still, folklorists of the late twentieth century have not budged. This lack of motivation in studying the use of folklore in burgeoning technology could conceivably rest within the ideologies bestowed upon folklore trainees prior the advent of the Internet and computerlore. Perhaps Richard Dorson's fears regarding the permeance of "fakelore" made the unverifiability of technologically based folklore a skeptical topic among new and old folklorists alike. Maybe it has been folklorists' favoritism toward the study of vanishing cultures and traditions, or "old-timey stuff" (as Henry Glassie used to call it in his graduate lectures).[23]

Or, perchance, could it be that no one scholar (or group of scholars) has stepped forward to guide the discipline into studying this field? There has been plenty of internal chatter about the Internet at folklore meetings, and the occasional journal article, but folklorists have not engaged in a greater dialogue with allied disciplines. Once folklorists liberate themselves from their self-imposed boundaries of scholastic inquiry, they will be able to complement or challenge the concepts put forth by scholars in fields such as sociology, communications, and popular-culture studies.

As Simon Bronner (2002) notes, the Internet is often thought of as mass culture par excellence, but it is hard to miss its qualities as a system of and a storehouse for folklore.[24] Still, the inherent intangibility of the Internet's interface may have made some ethnographers hesitant to engage the format. After all, Ben-Amos's classic definition of folklore assertively emphasizes that "folklore communication takes place in a situation in which people confront each other face to face and relate to each other directly" (Ben-Amos 1971, 12–13), yet he also declares that folklore "is the action that happens at [the time of the communicative event]" and, as such, "is an artistic action" (10). This is confusing when carried over into an Internet context. Clearly, communicative events take place, but the lack of face-to-face interactions contradicts the instinctual efforts of the ethnographer. These are only a few of the potential reasons why folklorists have neglected the Internet as a venue for scholastic inquiry.

It is important to note that not *all* folklorists turned a blind eye to the possibilities of studying folklore and technology.[25] Alan Dundes, one of folklore's greatest thinkers, knew that technology was a friend of the folklorist, not a foe. He wrote that "technology isn't stamping out folklore; rather it is becoming a vital factor in the transmission of folklore and it is providing an exciting source of inspiration for the generation of new folklore" (Dundes 1980, 17). Unfortunately, it appears that the majority of folklore scholars have missed this statement. While folk processes will exist so long as humans communicate and create, the academic discipline of folklore continues to be at risk of disappearing into other fields, either by way of assimilation or by a change in terminological boundaries. There has been internal bickering over the term "folklore" itself and its applicability as an ideological label for what folklorists study (Bendix 1998; Kirshenblatt-Gimblett 1998; Oring 1998). Regina Bendix notes that the field of folklore resists "semantic imprisonment" and thrives "on interdisciplinarity of method and thought" (Bendix 1998, 237). So there is still confusion as to what exactly constitutes folklore, and presumably the debate will continue so long as there are constituents to argue about it.

For the purposes of this book, it is important to define what, specifically, constitutes "folklore," particularly in an Internet context, in order to better frame the ideological underpinnings by which the authors and editor operate. Folklorists must be careful to carve out their niche in the scholarly dialogue so as not to confuse their approaches with those of anthropology or sociology. Not every issue involving electronic communication is necessarily a folklore issue, and we must equally examine the modifying terms that fall under the umbrella of "folklore" in an Internet context. What comprises vernacular expression? What do tradition, belief, legend, performance, and narrative mean in an Internet context? How does the Internet complicate notions of folk group, of audience, and of the dynamic, reflexive character of performance? As a mediatory agent, how does the Internet affect expression, engender unique folkloric material (and thus become a distinctive folk product itself), and reconfigure the nature of communication as a form of cultural maintenance and definition?

McClelland simplifies folklore by describing it as "communicative behavior whose primary characteristics . . . are that . . . it doesn't 'belong' to an individual or group . . . and in the modern context therefore transcends issues of intellectual property; and [that] . . . it is transmitted spontaneously, from one individual (or group of individuals) to another under certain conditions, frequently without regard for remuneration or return benefit. As it is transmitted, it often undergoes modification, according to the inclination of the retransmitter" (McClelland 2000, 184). This description weighs communication and transmission more heavily as essential components than do traditional notions of folklore, which celebrate the role of creativity and aesthetics. Nonetheless, folklore isn't limited to orality. Kirshenblatt-Gimblett notes that "folklore as a discipline has tended to conceive the everyday in largely aesthetic terms" (Kirshenblatt-Gimblett 1998, 308), pointing to Ben-Amos's definition of folklore as "artistic communication in small groups" (Ben-Amos 1971, 13) and the American Folklife Center's characterization as "community life and values, artfully expressed in myriad forms and interactions" (Hufford 1991, 1).[26] Elliott Oring puts it succinctly by saying that folklore "is about people—individuals and communities—and their aesthetic expression" (Oring 1998, 335). A reliance on *aesthetics* seems to place a stronger emphasis on tangibility as a measurement of what constitutes folklore than the terms *communication* and *transmission* might allow. Furthermore, it leaves room for prejudice—what one person may find beautiful or important conversely may seem ugly or frivolous to another. This is problematic.

We mustn't be afraid to challenge the boundaries of the folklore discipline. For too long we have regurgitated folkloristic studies or have been subsumed by other disciplines' methodologies. I propose a combination of the aforementioned definitions, as they all present limitations to the study of folklore on the Internet and oftentimes to other subdivisions of folkloristic inquiry. For this book, and hopefully beyond it, folklore should be considered to be the outward expression of creativity—in myriad forms and interactions—by individuals and their communities. The debate then falls to what constitutes *creativity* or even what constitutes *community*. *That* should be the job of the folklorist to argue cogently one way or another.[27] The resulting analytical construct, formed by the scholar in reaction to the character of folklore, is where a folklorist is needed for interpretation and indeed is qualified to comment.

It may be noted that *tradition* is curiously absent from this definition. As Simon Bronner notes, Dan Ben-Amos worried that tradition "prevented the folklorist's subject from expanding to emergent performances in mass culture" (Bronner 2002, 30). I share this concern.[28] Robert Glenn Howard reminds us that "what is essential about folkloric expression is not a 'traditional' origin. Instead, it is . . . 'continuities and consistencies' that allow a specific community to perceive such expression as traditional, local, or community generated" (Howard 2008a, 201).[29] A caveat worth mentioning is that my definition risks being conceived of as too broad, a longstanding problem in separating folklore from allied disciplines. However, I submit that folklore is empowered by its diversity; this definition is purposefully inclusive to capitalize on that strength of the discipline.[30]

If my definition may stand, then what merits folkloristic study? William Wells Newell believed that "technology, specifically print, produces the social distinction between high and low that generates folklore," and further posited that "genuine folklore" is lore that escapes print (Newell 1883, v). But we mustn't forget that print promoted folklore and allowed folklorists to "constitute the oral in relation to a distinctive technology of detachment and extension" (Kirshenblatt-Gimblett 1998, 309). The Internet is the new "print" technology, duplicating our materials from the physical field and transferring them (though not necessarily always altering them) into an electronic vernacular. The result is similar to the way that printed versions of folklore originally stimulated oral tradition in the past.[31] The Internet does not diminish the potency of folklore; instead, it acts as a folkloric conduit. "Electronic messages are neither a playscript nor a transcript . . . They *are* the event," writes Kirshenblatt-Gimblett (1995, 74; emphasis in original).

Benedict Anderson (1991) argues that technology can bring the vernacular into sight, thus facilitating community culture and promoting nationalism—traditional byproducts and correlates of folklore. The Internet has altered established notions of social identity, which has made stigmatizing constraints such as gender and race less relevant than they are in the physical world (McClelland 2000, 182). One must then ask, has this been a positive thing? I believe it has been. Due to its inclusivity, the Internet has helped to re-facilitate the spread of folklore through electronic conduits. Robert Thompson points out that "we have really returned here, in spite of the centralization of technology, to the old-fashioned definition of what folk culture used to be . . . We have these jokes and stories that will never see the printed page that exist only as glowing dots of phosphorous. It's not word-of-mouth folk culture but word-of-modem culture" (Grimes 1992, C14, quoted in Kirshenblatt-Gimblett 1996, 50).[32]

With regard to the burgeoning "telectronic age," John Dorst, in 1990, worried that "our discursive practices as folklorists do not equip us very well to deal with these unprecedented and complex conditions of cultural production" (Dorst 1990, 189). This may have been true 20 years ago, but the Internet has fundamentally changed the world we live in today and has been absorbed into the everyday life of folklorists of all generations. It is not a foreign commodity; it is a tool of cultural production that we utilize on a daily basis. As Howard notes, Dorst recognized "the capacity for network communication to blend vernacular and institutional modes of communication in ways that frustrated distinctions between 'folk' and mass media" (Howard 2008a, 192). This blending has been problematic for ethnographers, as the Internet's "field" is sometimes construed as foreign to them. It is difficult to find one's bearings at times. Nevertheless, the cyberfield is increasingly engaging humans despite its liminal state.

While the remoteness of the Internet may seem unappealing to the folklorist, Regina Bendix reminds us that "the field has never confined itself to 'remoteness,' and that its most interesting and least dogmatic thinkers have always found the ubiquity of expressive culture (across time, space, class) most intriguing" (Bendix 1998, 243). Folklore continues on the Internet whether we examine it or not,[33] so it is practical to study folklore in an Internet context. We must rethink the topics that have previously captured our interests and contemplate their Internet correlates. Perhaps some folklorists fear that the Internet will undermine the credibility of their work or negatively impact the content of their research, but it should be noted that "new technologies do not necessarily displace, replace, or eliminate earlier ones. They alter the relations among them and incorporate one another—with far-reaching effects" (Kirshenblatt-Gimblett 1998, 310). In the fraction of a second it takes for the human brain to send a command to the index finger, a single transmission of text can be distributed to potentially thousands, even millions of people. Internet users are frequently participating in many interesting folkloric activities online. Chain letters, "end of the Internet" websites, and forwarded humor are all ubiquitous. The Internet's proclivity for pseudonymous interaction and the ease with which texts can be transmitted make it the ideal location, instead of oral and journalistic venues, for the resurfacing of narrative texts.

So let's look at online narratives for a moment. By nature, e-mail hoaxes and forwarded humor cannot exist without the Internet, as they are exclusive to this venue. Through the microcosm of topical humor, Bill Ellis notes that "traditionally, folklore has been seen as a localized phenomenon . . . While previous collections from before 1987 stressed oral tradition, the anonymity of frequently forwarded messages has quickly made this the preferred mode of circulating topical humor," further adding that the "increased internationalism of email conduits now makes it normal, even commonplace, to exchange impressions and reactions across continental and even linguistic barriers . . . Comparing the content and form of [topical humor] to previous oral-based collections may reveal some significant ways in which the Internet has impacted the folk process" (Ellis 2001, section 4). In this regard, Daryl Cumber Dance holds that due to its contemporary accessibility, "techlore" has supplanted the paperwork empire as one of the most popular new forms of folklore: "With the advent of E-mail, pieces that were formerly copied and circulated are now sent with one click of the mouse to a long list of one's associates—who often send them on to other groups of acquaintances" (Dance 2002, 647). With topical humor, Liisi Laineste adds that "collecting jokes on the Internet is becoming . . . unavoidable" (Laineste 2003, 93). In a research setting, then, the text becomes both a primary and a secondary document, depending on the researcher's inclinations for its use.

In the pre-Internet age, one may have seen chain letters or text sprites in the form of letters sent pyramid scheme-like to random addresses or as a component of computer-lore or Xeroxlore (Dundes 1965; Dundes and Pagter 1975, 1987, 1996; Fox 1983). The Internet provides an anonymous medium for web users to quickly disseminate information, which often leads to a more authentic performance of the user's true self (Bargh, McKenna, and Fitzsimons 2002). In this sense, the Internet is an ideal channel for the transmission of folk narratives, due to its anonymity and efficiency in the speedy dissemination of ideas. For researchers, the electronic transmissions of narratives provide a greater paper trail to test out theorizations on the role of conduits in narrative transference. In their oral context, legends are richly evocative of society's fears, hopes, anxieties, and prejudices, and folklorists decode these narratives to reveal and analyze the cultural attitudes expressed within. The Internet provides a new opportunity for us to study legends and their subsidiaries, such as chain letters and e-mail hoaxes. While orally transmitted legends convey societal fears and prejudices in coded language, electronically transmitted narratives express these sentiments more abrasively, due to the sender's anonymity (Bargh, McKenna, and Fitzsimons 2002; Blank 2007; Eichhorn 2001; Fernback 2003; Kibby 2005).

Folk groups are readily identifiable on the Internet, as evidenced by chat forums, blogs, online political activity, fan web pages, and a plethora of other interrelated concepts. New traditions are being forged in online communities, and web lingo—emerging in such forms as net-derived lingo (see netlingo.com), wiki-based Internet vocabulary databases like urbandictionary.com, or the communal folk wisdom of online discussion groups—demonstrates the uniqueness of Internet expression.[34] Of course, these assertions are complicated by a lack of empirical data and physical connectivity between the researcher and his informant. As Barbara Kirshenblatt-Gimblett has contemplated, "What do terms like *group* or *community* mean when strangers at computer terminals at the far ends of the world type messages to each other? . . . The electronic vernacular is neither speech nor writing as we have known it, but something in between, and increasingly, with the convergence of technologies, it is multimedia" (Kirshenblatt-Gimblett 1998, 284; emphasis in original).

The digital world is paradoxically familiar, due to its governing social dynamics, and simultaneously foreign, due to its virtual format. The ethnographer faces many challenges that must be taken into consideration with the Internet. Milton Shatzer and Thomas Lindlof contend that ethnographers "cannot make adequate sense out of communication" without the ability to observe nonverbal behavioral cues, noting that e-mail and other online communications bypass the social pecking orders imposed in group interaction, such as eye contact, seating arrangements, and characteristics such as "gender, race, expertise, or organizational position" (Lindlof and Shatzer 1998, 178).[35] Coming from the perspective of folklore studies, I disagree. It is foolish to become fixated solely on the subconscious or nonverbal processes of communication. Is cyberethnography illegitimate because it equalizes the social statuses of its users? By ignoring cyberethnographic data, aren't we discounting a very important social dynamic that is taking place? We should be interested in how people express themselves, in whatever manner that occurs. Admonishing cyberethnography for its lack of physicality limits the scope of the researcher's analysis and is narrow-minded. While an expression may appear differently in the online world than it does in the physical world, there is room for analysis on the distinguishing characteristics between the two.

Internet scholar Denise Carter mentions that ethically, "cyberethnography is similar to conventional ethnography because the four main moral obligations of dealing with human subject research are the same: the principle of non-maleficence, the protection of anonymity, the confidentiality of data, and the obtaining of informed consent" (Carter 2005, 152). Moreover, communication "in the absence of face-to-face interaction and at a distance is as old as the circulation of objects . . . and the transmission of signals" (Kirshenblatt-Gimblett 1996, 21). As I have suggested before, the "lure of the foreignness of the field may be [a reason why we resist] the Internet as an appropriate place to conduct fieldwork. After all . . . conducting fieldwork 'in the field' is a tradition of the folklore discipline itself. However, as times change, our profession must progress accordingly" (Blank 2007, 21). It is undeniable that the psychological identification of place has been forged in the online format. With this in mind, I have posited that the Internet's "field" cannot be separated from the traditional field to which folklorists are accustomed. While there are fundamental differences between the two— specifically, that the former is virtual and the latter, physical—they are bound by common themes.[36] Both have folk groups, customs, lingo and dialects, neighborhoods, crimes, relationships, games, discussion groups, displays of emotion, banking, commerce, and various other forms of communication and education (Blank 2007).

It is important to realize that just because the Internet is virtual, or "doesn't exist" as McClelland (2000) contends, it still has an inherent base in the real world. The fact remains that there is a human behind everything that takes place online, and this is where the folklorist's fieldwork on the Internet should begin. We must ask ourselves, how do we interact with the computer as ethnographers and as participants? Who are the folk in cyberspace (the cyberfolk, if you will)? What makes them different from the traditional folk? What are the constraints or exigencies that dictate how they carry themselves in an Internet context? When we begin to answer these questions, we can then make a case for what constitutes vernacular expression and how these expressions evince creativity or traditional components. Howard says that norms and forms can be properly termed *vernacular* when they "signal local or 'home born' qualities of a particular human communication." He further asserts that vernacularity "can only emerge into meaning by being seen as distinct from the mass, the official, and the institutional" and argues that "there is a class of online discourse that is properly termed 'vernacular' because it invokes characteristics that are recognized as distinct from those recognized as 'institutional,'"[37] adding that while "this conception might frustrate our desires to rigidly locate discrete documents that are amateur or professional, traditional or mass mediated, its flexibility provides the theoretical language necessary for speaking about the inextricably intertwined nature of public and private, personal and commercial, individual and group in the communications that new technologies have made possible" (Howard 2008a, 194–95).[38] The vernacular comes to have meaning when it is alien to some institution (Glassie 1999; Howard 2005). Scholars may look at the same things, and draw the same conclusions, but they report their findings in their own discipline's terminology. Folklore is too important for that. We *are* the folk—as participants, as scholars, and as citizens. Our insight is needed.

Richard Bauman discusses the traditional concept of the homogeneous folk society as imposing a set of blinders on folklorists, skewing their attention away from conditions under which differences of identity gave shape to the social use of folklore (Bauman 1972, 1983, 1992). I believe that institutional hegemony runs the risk of imposing similar blinders on the scope of folkloristic inquiry. As scholars, we mustn't neglect technology and mass culture. "Mass culture uses folk culture," writes Kirshenblatt-Gimblett, and "folk culture mutates in a world of technology" (Kirshenblatt-Gimblett 1998, 307).[39] She further notes that "the very technologies that threaten to displace oral traditions are also the instruments for preserving them" (Kirshenblatt-Gimblett 1995, 70). The Internet is changing the game for folklorists and allied scholars; moreover, it is fundamentally changing culture and the way we should think about it (Putnam 2000). "The electronic inscription and reproduction of folklore forms merely epitomizes and makes especially visible the wholesale transformation of social and material relations that characterizes our historical moment" (Dorst 1990, 183).

The Internet has shifted the social constructions of community, often taking on its own unique characteristics and modes of expressions. Participatory media, notes Howard, offer "powerful new channels through which the vernacular can express its alterity" (Howard 2008a, 192). Creativity is at the center of folkloristic inquiry, and the manifestations of online identity formation, artistic expression, folk religion, and the social dynamics of community construction are all important venues for analysis.[40] However, as Howard also notes, "there is no 'pure' or finally 'authentic' vernacular. Instead, the vernacular needs the institutional from which to distinguish itself . . . no pure vernacularity exists, only degrees of hybridity" (Howard 2008a, 203; see also Howard 1997, 2001, 2005; Lawless 1998). Christine Hine addresses this point: "Ethnography of the [I]nternet can, then, usefully be about mobility between contexts of production and use, and between online and offline, and it can creatively deploy forms of engagement to look at how these sites are socially constructed and at the same time are social conduits" (Hine 2009, 11). For Richard Bauman, "members of particular groups or social categories may exchange folklore with each other on the basis of shared identity, or with others, on the basis of differential identity" (Bauman 1972, 38). Couldn't this extrapolation be applied to a folkloristic study of the Internet? It may be easy to find a text on a venue like the Internet, but the context may be difficult to ascertain. This is a challenge that folklorists can and must overcome as semiotics and the other cultural processes filtered through the Internet demand our attention (Mechling 1993).

In building off of these ruminations, *Folklore and the Internet* hopes to widen the dialogue about the Internet as both an ethnographic field and an area of folkloristic inquiry. This book is about the intersection of folklore—in all of its multifaceted incarnations—and the Internet. More importantly, the volume attempts to use a folkloristic perspective to critically examine and contribute to the literature on the sociocultural and performative nature of the Internet. Many of the topics traditionally explored by folklorists—such as humor, expression, tradition, narrative transmission, commemoration, religion, and ritual—have taken on new or modified lives in the digital world. The new essays comprising this book will explore the depth and flexibility of the Internet as a viable site of ethnography and scholarship, in addition to its relevance as a host for identity and communal expression and as a purveyor of various narratives and beliefs, ranging from topical humor to apocalyptic hyperbole.

Notes

1. The ethnographic research I was referring to at the time revolved around collecting the humorous vernacular responses to the death of Michael Jackson on June 25, 2009 that colorfully circulated both online and in oral traditions thereafter. This work was eventually published in the journal *Midwestern Folklore* (Blank 2009c) and later expanded upon in *The Last Laugh* (Blank 2013a, 83–98).

2. Additionally, this scholar demanded: "How can you claim to have a legitimate informant if you don't know who they 'really' are as a person in their day-to-day lives?" Such concerns were common as researching folklore and the Internet gradually garnered more widespread acceptance within the discipline. The evolution of a field is never without its strains.

3. During my early years of graduate school, most of my professors had no vested interest in my research on folklore and the Internet, which was then perceived as a "fringe" area of inquiry. Thus, in the context of *this* fateful interaction—where my work and core interests in folklore were under direct attack—I already knew that I was in the minority, albeit a growing one. Therefore, I chose to forgo arguing with an unconvertible audience. In that moment, my interests painted me as a misguided, idealistic graduate student who had just been "schooled" by an accomplished folklorist. Fortunately, as time has proven, those concerns about the merits of folkloristic fieldwork on the Internet proved unfounded. In addition to the scholars cited in Blank (2009a, 2009b), see also Blank (2012a, 2013a, 2013b, 2014, 2015); Buccitelli (2012, 2013); Ellis (2012); Frank (2004, 2011); Howard (2011); Kaplan (2013); and Miller (2012), among others, for additional applications of and theoretical work on cyberethnography in the study of folk culture and human behavior online (see also Blascovich and Bailenson 2011). And one final point in recalling this interaction: if there is one thing I have learned in my college teaching career, it is that the chance to foster the intellectual development of motivated and imaginative students is a rare gift that should always be undertaken with pride, respect, and unmatched encouragement—even when dealing with "fringe" areas of inquiry. Innovation will be the only thing to reliably perpetuate the investigation of new and evolving folklore in the twenty-first century.

4. Likewise, I should note that my colleague's claims further reveal the prevailing notion of the day: that folklore surfaces most authentically in face-to-face

settings and via oral transmission—a contention that has seen its share of proponents and challenges in recent years. To illustrate this dichotomy, see Bill Ivey's 2007 AFS Presidential Address (Ivey 2011) and Howard and Blank's (2013) ensuing response for a pointed critique of anti-modern sentiments in folkloristics such as the ones espoused by Ivey. See also Blank and Howard (2013) for additional perspectives on folklore, tradition, and modernity. And see Blank (2009a, 8, 10–11)—also reprinted in this monograph—for specific discussion about folklorists wrestling with notions of the "field" and fieldwork, including what renders the endeavor legitimate.

5. I am eternally grateful to *Folklore and the Internet* contributors Simon J. Bronner, Robert Dobler, Russell Frank, Gregory Hansen, Robert Glenn Howard, Lynne S. McNeill, Elizabeth Tucker, and William Westerman, and to John Alley and Michael Spooner of Utah State University Press for making the book a reality. It was a real treasure to work with all of them.

6. Meaning that the well-documented expressive patterns of face-to-face communication were observably circulating in virtualized form, even as Internet-derived folkloric material disseminated in the physical world, thereby hybridizing folklore.

7. For specific discussion of updating and expanding upon *Folklore and the Internet* within the introduction, see Blank (2012b, 12–14).

8. See Bronner (1988, 2004) for supplementary description and folkloristic applications of praxis.

9. Although individual academic publishers certainly vary in review and processing efficiency, a recent study shows that the *average* publication delay period for humanities journals—which would include folklore studies—extends to eighteen months, or twice as long as journals in the chemistry field (Björk and Solomon 2013). Again, this calculation does not include the length of time it takes for a scholar to prepare his or her research and writing before initial submission. Realistically, then, a single humanities publication could easily take over two years (or more) to produce from start to finish—a considerable lag when documenting folklore in the twenty-first century.

10. I do not wish to suggest that a so-called "antiquated" publication is inherently without value. If nothing else, dated Internet research provides tremendous insight into the historical arguments, earlier expressive modes, and derivative patterns of repetition and variation that collectively inform and populate the folklore of the digital age. My main goal here is to accentuate the difficult task of producing cutting edge research on contemporary folklore in light of slow-moving publication queues that potentially limit a work's freshness and contextual relevancy when significantly delayed.

11. This is not to say that are no limitations to technologically mediated communication as a conduit for folkloric expression. While I tend to be optimistic, several scholars have raised some very valid points about the downsides of

computer-mediated communication. See Mayer-Schönberger (2009) and Turkle (2011) for two relatively recent publications that provide especially compelling argumentation and case studies in this regard.

12. Consider the fact that the average age in which a child receives their first mobile phone in the United States is around nine and a half, with kids living in single-parent households acquiring them even earlier; meanwhile, teenagers send an average of over three thousand text messages per month (Clark 2013, viii; Madden et al. 2013; see also Lenhart et al. 2010). Although these figures have likely changed since the time of their original collection, the widespread adoption of technologically mediated communication platforms among youths nevertheless indicates a significant divergence in how the upcoming generation differs socially from other digital natives (see Blank 2013a, xix–xx; McNeill 2009).

13. "Creepypasta" is a narrative genre of Internet folklore in which individuals write, copy, modify, and/or post short horror stories intended to innocuously frighten or disturb readers for fun.

14. Photoshopped humor has been a staple of vernacular expression in online settings for well over a decade (Blank 2013a, 44–55; Ellis 2002; Foster 2012; Frank 2004, 2011). In times of social anxiety and political strain, these user-manipulated images have come to serve as visual gestures of dissent, pushing back against emotionally hegemonic institutions like the mass media, or through the deployment of humorous rhetoric, symbolically chiding institutional authority figures when their actions betray the expectations societally bestowed upon their offices of power (see Blank 2013a). To some extent, folklore on (and from) the Internet has often been discernible through its more visually oriented themes of expression (Bronner 2009; see also Foote 2007; Hathaway 2005; Kuipers 2005). Internet scholar Limor Shifman similarly observes that online, "the visual seems to triumph over the verbal . . . Most of the texts are image-based and the new types of Internet humor tend to be visual" (Shifman 2007, 204).

15. See also Shirky (2008, 109–42, 271–72). Examples of wiki-based websites include *Wikipedia*, *Encyclopedia Dramatica*, and to a lesser extent, *Urban Dictionary* (see Kaplan 2013, 132–34). Browse to http://en.wikipedia.org/wiki/List_of_wikis for a larger sampling.

16. The hybridization of folk culture has increasingly been the subject of recent folkloristic scholarship. Key examples include Blank (2013b, 2015); Buccitelli (2013); Cocq (2013); Howard (2008a, 2008b, 2015); and Thompson (2011). For broader ruminations on hybridity, see also Aldred (2010); Blank (2012b, 3–4, 6–8, 12); Bronner (2009); de Souza e Silva (2006); Foote (2007); Hathaway (2005); Jenkins (2008); Kapchan and Strong (1999); McNeill (2012); and Stross (1999). Without question, evaluating the complex dynamics of hybridity is critically important to understanding folklore in the digital age—even as the cognitive distinction between corporeality and virtuality becomes progressively indiscernible and obsolete.

17. Here again we have found for the folklorist "a truly contemporary subject, one that is not just *in* the present, but truly *of* the present" (Kirshenblatt-Gimblett 1995, 70, emphasis in original; see also Blank 2009a, 17). Still, I stand by my earlier pronouncement that "Not every issue involving electronic communication is necessarily a folklore issue" (Blank 2009a, 5). It is the responsibility of the folklorist to identify and pursue worthwhile research topics involving technologically mediated communication.

18. There have been some thoughtful writings on the history of the Internet. See Okin (2005) or, for a brief treatment, Bermejo (2007, 57–73). While *Folklore and the Internet* is interested in a folkloristic approach to Internet studies, a few works from allied scholars bear further examination for broad overviews of computer-mediated studies: Healy (1997); Krawczyk-Wasilewska (2006); Kuntsman (2004); Silver, Massanari, and Jones (2006); Weber and Dixon (2007); and Wood and Smith (2005).

19. Jennings's (1990) *The Devouring Fungus* may have been one of the first attempts to examine the folkloric aspects of the shifting currents in technology from the computer/Xeroxlore age to the possibilities presented by the interconnectivity of the Internet. If nothing else, it's an interesting timepiece about changes in folkloric transmission at the end of the 1980s, particularly since it examines "tales from the computer age" only a few years before the modern Internet exploded onto the scene. See also Sproull and Kiesler 1992.

20. This originally appeared in an electronic version in 1993. See also Shea (1994) for a further treatment of the phenomenon that Rheingold is referencing.

21. Full access to past and new issues of *Folklore Forum* is available at http://folkloreforum.net. Archived issues can be found at https://scholarworks.iu.edu/dspace/handle/2022/1168.

22. This isn't a criticism so much as it is a disappointment for the lack of interest in the subject matter from seasoned folklore veterans and graduate students. In soliciting entries for this book, it was particularly difficult to find contributors whose primary research interests revolved around the intersection of folklore and the Internet, but many people had a secondary or peripheral interest in the subject matter. Hopefully this will change soon!

23. My thanks to Libby Tucker for sharing her memories of this.

24. Bronner's assertion was expanded upon via personal communication with the author in September 2008.

25. As cited earlier, several scholars have made a name for themselves examining folklore and technology, such as John Dorst, Robert Glenn Howard, and Barbara Kirshenblatt-Gimblett, among a handful of others.

26. See also Marvin (1995).

27. For example, I often ask myself, does a locale require "tradition" in order be considered a "community"? This is a question that could be further examined in great detail by folklorists.

28. See Ben-Amos (1972) for further contemplations on the limitations posed by the inclusion of "tradition" in defining folklore.

29. See also Baym (1993) and especially Georges and Jones (1995), where the idea of "continuities and consistencies" originates. Additionally, see Howard (2008a).

30. My thanks to Robert Glenn Howard for his assistance in clarifying this point.

31. For an example of how sixteenth-century folksong collectors' performances benefited from, and were not diminished by, print, see Kirshenblatt-Gimblett (1998, 309–10).

32. That said, in chapter 1 of this volume Simon J. Bronner argues that there are distinguishable "folk" and "elite" cultures on the Internet.

33. Arjun Appadurai (1986) explores this concept in greater detail.

34. For example, urbandictionary.com is interesting because it presents slang and linguistic culture not only from the Internet, but also from the physical world. It can thus be seen as a facilitator in the relationship between the offline and online world. This should be of particular interest to folklorists who study topical humor, word play, and verbal dueling, as this venue is moderated by anonymous contributors from across the globe and features a combination of narrative lore found in multiple cultural venues.

35. Jan Roush astutely synthesizes some of the main ethical and practical considerations folklorists face in utilizing the Internet for conducting fieldwork: "Does fieldwork . . . have to be conducted in face-to-face interviews in order to be defined as fieldwork, or is any medium sufficient? . . . How does an effaced interview conducted through electronic mail or real-time Chat groups alter the performance, the context of the collecting? Further, since Internet access is for now limited to a privileged few participants, how representative of vernacular culture is this type of fieldwork? . . . [W]hat assurances does the collector have that the informants are actually who they say they are, an issue particularly crucial in collecting certain types of lore like gender lore? . . . How does the collector obtain valid consent forms? Further, if consent forms are transmitted through say, the medium of e-mail, can this collected information legally be archived?" (Roush 1997, 45). These are all valid questions to ponder, and I encourage folklorists to contemplate them further.

36. I believe this assertion is supported by other scholars in allied disciplines. Citing over three years of ethnographic research, Denise Carter reported that her informants found their online community "just another place to meet friends" and that "many of the friendships formed . . . are routinely being moved offline." Consequently, Carter concludes, "the basic tenets of online friendship appear to be impossible to separate from the traditional everyday concept of friendship itself" (Carter 2005, 164). This supports my belief that the authenticity of the data collected online is as valid as data collected in person (Blank 2007).

Of course, the question remains as to whether the Internet increases a person's likelihood to interact as a non-authentic self, but as Christine Hine so precisely stated: "The point for the ethnographer is not to bring some external criterion for judging whether it is safe to believe what informants say, but rather to come to understand how it is that informants judge authenticity" (Hine 2000, 49). For a thorough discussion of authenticity as it relates to folklore studies, see Bendix (1997).

37. This assertion is supported by the arguments presented by Simon J. Bronner in chapter 1 of this volume.

38. For a review of the origins of the term "vernacular," see Howard (2005, 327–28).

39. See also Bronner (2004); Dégh (1994); and Kirshenblatt-Gimblett (1983) for a deeper discussion of mass culture and its influence on and interaction with aspects of folklore. Howard (2008a, 200–1) also reviews the literature on folklore and the mass media quite appropriately and effectively.

40. John McDowell has utilized the Internet as a medium in his F351 folklore classes at Indiana University ("The Folklore of Student Life"). Through archival data and student fieldwork, he has pieced together an impressive website that displays a sample of Indiana University folklore from the past and present. I encourage readers to visit it at http://www.indiana.edu/~f351jmcd/. I think that this site is yet another demonstration of how we can think of the Internet not only as a tool for folkloristic inquiry, but as a comrade in the presentation of our work and methods. For a thoughtful report on the concerns folklorists may have with these types of digital media, see Underberg (2006).

References

Aldred, B. Grantham. 2010. "Identity in 10,000 Pixels: LiveJournal Userpics and Fractured Selves in Web 2.0." *New Directions in Folklore* 8, no. 1/2: 6–35.

Anderson, Benedict. 1991. *Imagined Communities: Reflections on the Origins and Spread of Nationalism.* New York: Verso Press.

Appadurai, Arjun. 1986. *The Social Life of Things: Commodities in Cultural Perspective.* Cambridge: Cambridge University Press.

Bargh, John A., Katelyn Y. A. McKenna, and Grainne M. Fitzsimons. 2002. "Can You See the Real Me? Activation and Expression of the 'True Self' on the Internet." *Journal of Social Issues* 58 (1): 33–48. http://dx.doi.org/10.1111/1540-4560.00247.

Bauman, Richard. 1972. "Differential Identity and the Social Base of Folklore." In *Toward New Perspectives in Folklore*, ed. Américo Paredes and Richard Bauman, 31–41. Austin: University of Texas Press.

Bauman, Richard. 1983. "Folklore and the Forces of Modernity." *Folklore Forum* 16: 153–58.

Bauman, Richard, ed. 1992. *Folklore, Cultural Performances, and Popular Entertainments: A Communications-Centered Handbook.* New York: Oxford University Press.

Bauman, Richard, and Charles L. Briggs. 2003. *Voices of Modernity: Language Ideologies and the Politics of Inequality.* Cambridge: Cambridge University Press. http://dx.doi.org/10.1017/CBO9780511486647.

Baym, Nancy K. 1993. "Interpreting Soap Operas and Creating Community: Inside a Computer-Mediated Fan Culture." *Journal of Folklore Research* 30:143–77.

Baym, Nancy K. 2010. *Personal Connections in the Digital Age.* Malden, MA: Polity Press.

Ben-Amos, Dan. 1971. "Toward a Definition of Folklore in Context." *Journal of American Folklore* 84 (331): 3–15. http://dx.doi.org/10.2307/539729.

Ben-Amos, Dan. 1972. "Toward a Definition of Folklore in Context." In *Toward New Perspectives in Folklore*, ed. Américo Paredes and Richard Bauman, 3–15. Austin: University of Texas Press.

Bendix, Regina. 1997. *In Search of Authenticity: The Formation of Folklore Studies.* Madison: University of Wisconsin Press.

Bendix. 1998. "Of Names, Professional Identities, and Disciplinary Futures." *Journal of American Folklore* 111 (441): 235–46. http://dx.doi.org/10.2307/541309.

Bermejo, Fernando. 2007. *The Internet Audience: Constitution & Measurement.* New York: Peter Lang.

Blank, Trevor J. 2007. "Examining the Transmission of Urban Legends: Making the Case for Folklore Fieldwork on the Internet." *Folklore Forum* 37: 15–26.

Blank, Trevor J. 2009a. "Toward a Conceptual Framework for the Study of Folklore and the Internet." In *Folklore and the Internet: Vernacular Expression in a Digital World,* ed. Trevor J. Blank, 1–20. Logan: Utah State University Press.

Blank, Trevor J., ed. 2009b. *Folklore and the Internet: Vernacular Expression in a Digital World.* Logan: Utah State University Press.

Blank, Trevor J. 2009c. "Moonwalking in the Digital Graveyard: Diversions in Oral and Electronic Humor Regarding the Death of Michael Jackson." *Midwestern Folklore* 35, no. 2: 71–90.

Blank, Trevor J, ed. 2012a. *Folk Culture in the Digital Age: The Emergent Dynamics of Human Interaction.* Logan: Utah State University Press.

Blank, Trevor J. 2012b. "Pattern in the Virtual Folk Culture of Computer-Mediated Communication." In *Folk Culture in the Digital Age: The Emergent Dynamics of Human Interaction,* ed. Trevor J. Blank, 1–24. Logan: Utah State University Press.

Blank, Trevor J. 2013a. *The Last Laugh: Folk Humor, Celebrity Culture, and Mass-Mediated Disasters in the Digital Age.* Madison: University of Wisconsin Press.

Blank, Trevor J. 2013b. "Hybridizing Folk Culture: Toward a Theory of New Media and Vernacular Discourse." *Western Folklore* 72, no. 2: 105–30.

Blank, Trevor J. 2014. "Giving the 'Big Ten' a Whole New Meaning: Tasteless Humor and the Response to the Penn State Sexual Abuse Scandal." In *The Folkloresque: Reframing Folklore in a Popular Culture World,* ed. Michael Dylan Foster and Jeffrey Tolbert. Logan: Utah State University Press, forthcoming.

Blank, Trevor J. 2015. "Faux Your Entertainment: Amazon.com Product Reviews as a Locus of Digital Performance." In "Folklore and the Internet." Special issue, *Journal of American Folklore,* forthcoming.

Blank, Trevor J., and Robert Glenn Howard, eds. 2013. *Tradition in the Twenty-First Century: Locating the Role of the Past in the Present.* Logan: Utah State University Press.

Blascovich, Jim, and Jeremy Bailenson. 2011. *Infinite Reality: Avatars, Eternal Life, New Worlds, and the Dawn of the Virtual Revolution.* New York: William Morrow.

Björk, Bo-Christer, and David Solomon. 2013. "The Publishing Delay in
    Scholarly Peer-Reviewed Journals." *Journal of Informetrics* 7, no. 4:
    914–23. Open access version: http://openaccesspublishing.org/oa11/
    article.pdf.

Bronner, Simon J. [1986] 2004. *Grasping Things: Folk Material Culture and
    Mass Society in America*. Lexington: University Press of Kentucky.

Bronner, Simon J. 1988. "Art, Performance, and Praxis: The Rhetoric of Con-
    temporary Folklore Studies." *Western Folklore* 47, no. 2: 75–101.

Bronner, Simon J. 2002. *Folk Nation: Folklore in the Creation of American Tradi-
    tion*. Wilmington, DE: Scholarly Resources.

Bronner, Simon J. 2009. "Digitizing and Virtualizing Folklore." In *Folklore and
    the Internet: Vernacular Expression in a Digital World*, ed. Trevor J. Blank,
    21–66. Logan: Utah State University Press.

Buccitelli, Anthony Bak. 2012. "Performance 2.0: Observations toward a The-
    ory of the Digital Performance of Folklore." In *Folk Culture in the Digital
    Age: The Emergent Dynamics of Human Interaction*, ed. Trevor J. Blank,
    60–84. Logan: Utah State University Press.

Buccitelli, Anthony Bak. 2013. "Virtually a Local: Folk Geography, Discourse,
    and Local Identity on the Geospatial Web." *Western Folklore* 72, no. 1:
    29–59.

Carter, Denise. 2005. "Living in Virtual Communities: An Ethnography of
    Human Relationships in Cyberspace." *Information Communication and
    Society* 8 (2): 148–67. http://dx.doi.org/10.1080/13691180500146235.

Chayko, Mary. 2008. *Portable Communities: The Social Dynamics of Online and
    Mobile Connectedness*. Albany: State University of New York Press.

Clark, Lynn Schofield. 2013. *The Parent App: Understanding Families in the
    Digital Age*. Oxford, UK: Oxford University Press.

Cocq, Coppélie. 2013. "Anthropological Places, Digital Spaces, and Imaginary
    Scapes: Packaging a Digital Sámiland." *Folklore: The Journal of the Folk-
    lore Society* 124, no. 1: 1–14.

Dance, Daryl Cumber, ed. 2002. *From My People: 400 Years of African American
    Folklore*. New York: W. W. Norton.

de Souza e Silva, Adriana. 2006. "From Cyber to Hybrid: Mobile Technologies
    as Interfaces of Hybrid Spaces." *Space and Culture* 6, no. 3: 261–78.

Dégh, Linda. 1994. *American Folklore and the Mass Media*. Bloomington: Indi-
    ana University Press.

Dobler, Robert. 2009. "Ghosts in the Machine: Mourning the MySpace Dead."
    In *Folklore and the Internet: Vernacular Expression in a Digital World*, ed.
    Trevor J. Blank, 175–93. Logan: Utah State University Press.

Dorson, Richard M. 1972. "Introduction: Concepts of Folklore and Folklife
    Studies." In *Folklore and Folklife: An Introduction*, ed. Richard M. Dor-
    son, 1–50. Chicago: University of Chicago Press.

Dorst, John. 1990. "Tags and Burners, Cycles and Networks: Folklore in the Telectronic Age." *Journal of Folklore Research* 27:179–90.

Dundes, Alan. 1965. "On Computers and Folktales." *Western Folklore* 24 (3): 185–9. http://dx.doi.org/10.2307/1498073.

Dundes, Alan. 1980. *Interpreting Folklore*. Bloomington: Indiana University Press.

Dundes, Alan. 2005. "Folkloristics in the Twenty-First Century (AFS Invited Presidential Plenary Address, 2004)." *Journal of American Folklore* 118 (470): 385–408. http://dx.doi.org/10.1353/jaf.2005.0044.

Dundes, Alan, and Carl R. Pagter. 1975. *Urban Folklore from the Paperwork Empire*. Austin, TX: American Folklore Society.

Dundes, Alan, and Carl R. Pagter. 1987. *When You're Up to Your Ass in Alligators: More Urban Folklore from the Paperwork Empire*. Detroit: Wayne State University Press.

Dundes, Alan, and Carl R. Pagter. 1996. *Sometimes the Dragon Wins: Yet More Urban Folklore from the paperwork Empire*. Syracuse: Syracuse University Press.

Eichhorn, Kate. 2001. "Sites Unseen: Ethnographic Research in a Textual Community." *Qualitative Studies in Education* 14 (4): 565–78. http://dx.doi.org/10.1080/09518390110047075.

Ellis, Bill. 2001. "A Model for Collecting and Interpreting World Trade Center Disaster Jokes." *Newfolk: New Directions in Folklore* 5. http://www.temple.edu/english/isllc/newfolk/wtchumor.html.

Ellis, Bill. 2002. "Making a Big Apple Crumble: The Role of Humor in Constructing a Global Response to Disaster." *New Directions in Folklore* 6. http://hdl.handle.net/2022/6911.

Ellis, Bill. 2012. "Love and War and Anime Art: An Ethnographic Look at a Virtual Community of Collectors." In *Folk Culture in the Digital Age: The Emergent Dynamics of Human Interaction*, ed. Trevor J. Blank, 166–211. Logan: Utah State University Press.

Fernback, Jan. 2003. "Legends on the Net: An Examination of Computer-Mediated Communication as a Locus of Oral Culture." *New Media & Society* 5 (1): 29–45. http://dx.doi.org/10.1177/1461444803005001902.

Foote, Monica. 2007. "Userpicks: Cyber Folk Art in the Early 21st Century." *Folklore Forum* 37: 27–38.

Foster, Michael Dylan. 2012. "Photoshop Folklore and the 'Tourist Guy': Thoughts on the Diamond Format and the Possibilities of Mixed-Media Presentations." *New Directions in Folklore* 10, no. 1: 85–91. http://scholarworks.iu.edu/journals/index.php/ndif/article/view/1930/1907.

Fox, William. 1983. "Computerized Creation and Diffusion of Folkloric Materials." *Folklore Forum* 16: 5–20.

Frank, Russell. 2004. "When the Going Gets Tough, the Tough Go Photo-shopping: September 11 and the Newslore of Vengeance and Victim-ization." *New Media & Society* 6, no. 5: 633–58.

Frank, Russell. 2011. *Newslore: Contemporary Folklore on the Internet*. Jackson: University Press of Mississippi.

Fuller, Steve. 2002. *Social Epistemology*. Bloomington: Indiana University Press.

Georges, Robert A., and Michael Owen Jones. 1995. *Folkloristics: An Introduc-tion*. Bloomington: Indiana University Press.

Glassie, Henry. 1999. *Material Culture*. Bloomington: Indiana University Press.

Grimes, William. 1992. "Computer As a Cultural Tool: Chatter Mounts on Every Topic." *New York Times*, December 1, section C, 13–14.

Hafner, Katie, and Matthew Lyon. 1998. *Where Wizards Stay Up Late: The Origins of the Internet*. New York: Simon & Schuster.

Hathaway, Rosemary V. 2005. "'Life in the TV': The Visual Nature of 9/11 Lore and Its Impact on Vernacular Response." *Journal of Folklore Research* 42, no. 1: 33–56.

Healy, David. 1997. "Cyberspace and Place: The Internet As Middle Landscape on the Electronic Frontier." In *Internet Culture*, ed. David Porter, 55–69. New York: Routledge.

Hine, Christine. 2000. *Virtual Ethnography*. London: Sage.

Hine, Christine. 2009. "Question One: How Can Qualitative Internet Researchers Define the Boundaries of Their Projects?" In *Internet Inquiry: Conversations about Method*, ed. Annette N. Markham and Nancy K. Baym, 1–29. Los Angeles: Sage Publications.

Howard, Robert Glenn. 1997. "Apocalypse in Your In-Box: End Times Com-munication on the Internet." *Western Folklore* 56 (3/4): 295–315. http://dx.doi.org/10.2307/1500281.

Howard, Robert Glenn. 2000. "On-Line Ethnography of Dispensationalist Dis-course: Revealed versus Negotiated Truth." In *Religion on the Internet*, ed. Douglas Cowan and Jeffery K. Hadden, 225–246. New York: Elsevier.

Howard, Robert Glenn. 2001. "Passages Divinely Lit: Revelatory Vernacular Rhetoric on the Internet." PhD diss., University of Oregon.

Howard, Robert Glenn. 2005. "Toward a Theory of the World Wide Web Ver-nacular: The Case for Pet Cloning." *Journal of Folklore Research* 42 (3): 323–60. http://dx.doi.org/10.2979/JFR.2005.42.3.323.

Howard, Robert Glenn, and the Robert Glenn Howard. 2008a. "Electronic Hybridity: The Persistent Processes of the Vernacular Web." *Journal of American Folklore* 121 (480): 192–218. http://dx.doi.org/10.1353/jaf.0.0012.

Howard, Robert Glenn. 2008b. "The Vernacular Web of Participatory Media." *Critical Studies in Media Communication* 25 (5): 490–512. http://dx.doi.org/10.1080/15295030802468065.

Howard, Robert Glenn. 2011. *Digital Jesus: The Making of a New Christian Fundamentalist Community on the Internet.* New York: New York University Press.

Howard, Robert Glenn. 2015. "Why Digital Network Hybridity is the New Normal (Hey! Check This Stuff Out)." In "Folklore and the Internet." Special issue, *Journal of American Folklore*, forthcoming.

Howard, Robert Glenn, and Trevor J. Blank. 2013. "Living Traditions in a Modern World." In *Tradition in the Twenty-First Century: Locating the Role of the Past in the Present,* ed. Trevor J. Blank and Robert Glenn Howard, 1–21. Logan: Utah State University Press.

Hufford, Mary. 1991. *American Folklife: A Commonwealth of Cultures.* Washington, DC: American Folklife Center, Library of Congress.

Ivey, Bill. 2011. "Values and Value in Folklore (AFS Plenary Address, 2007)." *Journal of American Folklore* 124, no. 491: 6–18.

Jenkins, Henry. 2008 [2006]. *Convergence Culture: Where Old and New Media Collide.* New York: New York University Press.

Jennings, Karla. 1990. *The Devouring Fungus: Tales of the Computer Age.* New York: W.W. Norton.

Kapchan, Deborah A., and Pauline Turner Strong. 1999. "Theorizing the Hybrid." *Journal of American Folklore* 112, no. 445: 239–53.

Kaplan, Merrill. 2013. "Curation and Tradition on Web 2.0." In *Tradition in the Twenty-First Century: Locating the Role of the Past in the Present,* ed. Trevor J. Blank and Robert Glenn Howard, 123–48. Logan: Utah State University Press.

Kibby, Marjorie. 2005. "Email Forwardables: Folklore in the Age of the Internet." *New Media & Society* 7 (6): 770–90. http://dx.doi.org/10.1177/1461444805058161.

Kirshenblatt-Gimblett, Barbara. 1983. "The Future of Folklore Studies in America: The Urban Frontier." *Folklore Forum* 16: 175–234.

Kirshenblatt-Gimblett, Barbara. 1995. "From the Paperwork Empire to the Paperless Office: Testing the Limits of the 'Science of Tradition.'" In *Folklore Interpreted: Essays in Honor of Alan Dundes,* ed. Regina Bendix and Rosemary Levy Zumwalt, 69–92. New York: Garland.

Kirshenblatt-Gimblett, Barbara. 1996. "The Electronic Vernacular." In *Connected: Engagements with Media,* ed. George E. Marcus, 21–66. Chicago: University of Chicago Press.

Kirshenblatt-Gimblett, Barbara. 1998. "Folklore's Crisis." *Journal of American Folklore* 111 (441): 281–327. http://dx.doi.org/10.2307/541312.

Krawczyk-Wasilewska, Violetta. 2006. "E-Folklore in the Age of Globalization." *Fabula* 47 (3-4): 248–54. http://dx.doi.org/10.1515/FABL.2006.027.

Kuipers, Giselinde. 2005. "'Where Was King Kong When We Needed Him?' Public Discourse, Digital Disaster Jokes, and the Functions of Laughter after 9/11." *Journal of American Culture* 28, no. 1: 70–84.

Kuntsman, Adi. 2004. "Cyberethnography as Home-Work." *Anthropology Matters Journal* 6:1–10.

Laineste, Liisi. 2003. "Researching Humor on the Internet." *Folklore: An Electronic Journal of Folklore* 25. http://www.folklore.ee/folklore/vol25/humor.pdf.

Lawless, Elaine J. 1998. "*Ars Rhetorica en Communitas*: Reclaiming the Voice of Passionate Expression in Electronic Writing." *Rhetoric Review* 16 (2): 310–26. http://dx.doi.org/10.1080/07350199809389098.

Lenhart, Amanda, Rich Ling, Scott Campbell, and Kristin Purcell. 2010. "Teens and Mobile Phones." *Pew Research Internet Project.* http://www.pewinternet.org/2010/04/20/teens-and-mobile-phones.

Lindlof, Thomas R., and Milton J. Shatzer. 1998. "Media Ethnography in Virtual Space: Strategies, Limits, and Possibilities." *Journal of Broadcasting & Electronic Media* 42 (2): 170–89. http://dx.doi.org/10.1080/08838159809364442.

Madden, Mary, Amanda Lenhart, Maeve Duggan, Sandra Cortesi, and Urs Gasser. 2013. "Teens and Technology 2013." *Pew Research Center and the Berkman Center for Internet and Society at Harvard University.* http://www.pewinternet.org/files/old-media/Files/Reports/2013/PIP_TeensandTechnology2013.pdf.

Marvin, Lee-Ellen. 1995. "Spoof, Spam, Lurk, and Lag: The Aesthetics of Text-Based Virtual Realities." *Journal of Computer-Mediated Communication* 1 (2). http://onlinelibrary.wiley.com/journal/10.1111/(ISSN)1083-6101.

Mayer-Schönberger, Viktor. 2009. *Delete: The Virtue of Forgetting in the Digital Age.* Princeton, NJ: Princeton University Press.

McClelland, Bruce. 2000. "Online Orality: The Internet, Folklore, and Culture in Russia." In *Culture and Technology in New Europe: Civic Discourse in Transformation in Post-Communist Nations*, ed. Laura B. Lengel, 179–191. Stamford, CT: Ablex.

McLuhan, Eric, and Frank Zingrone, eds. 1996. *Essential McLuhan.* New York: Basic Books.

McNeill, Lynne S. 2009. "The End of the Internet: The Folk Response to the Provision of Infinite Choice." In *Folklore and the Internet: Vernacular Expression in a Digital World*, ed. Trevor J. Blank, 80–97. Logan: Utah State University Press.

McNeill, Lynne S. 2012. "Real Virtuality: Enhancing Locality by Enacting the Small World Theory." In *Folk Culture in the Digital Age: The Emergent Dynamics of Human Interaction*, ed. Trevor J. Blank, 85–97. Logan: Utah State University Press.

McNeill, Lynne S. 2013. "And the Greatest of These Is Tradition: The Folklorist's Toolbox in the Twenty-First Century." In *Tradition in the Twenty-First Century: Locating the Role of the Past in the Present*, ed.

Trevor J. Blank and Robert Glenn Howard, 174–85. Logan: Utah State University Press.

Mechling, Jay. 1993. "On Sharing Folklore and American Identity in a Multicultural Society." *Western Folklore* 52 (2/4): 271–89. http://dx.doi.org/10.2307/1500090.

Miller, Montana. 2012. "Face-to-Face with the Digital Folk: The Ethics of Fieldwork on Facebook." In *Folk Culture in the Digital Age: The Emergent Dynamics of Human Interaction*, ed. Trevor J. Blank, 212–32. Logan: Utah State University Press.

Newell, William Wells. 1883. *Games and Songs of American Children*. New York: Harper and Brothers.

Okin, J.R. 2005. *The Internet Revolution: The Not-for-Dummies Guide to the History, Technology, and Use of the Internet*. Winter Harbor, ME: Ironbound Press.

Oring, Elliott. 1998. "Anti Anti-'Folklore'.'." *Journal of American Folklore* 111 (441): 328–38. http://dx.doi.org/10.2307/541313.

Putnam, Robert D. 2000. *Bowling Alone: The Collapse and Revival of American Community*. New York: Simon & Schuster. http://dx.doi.org/10.1145/358916.361990.

Rheingold, Howard. 2000. *The Virtual Community: Homesteading on the Electronic Frontier*. Cambridge, MA: MIT Press. Electronic version (1993) available at http://www.rheingold.com/vc/book/2.html.

Roush, Jan. 1997. "Folklore Fieldwork on the Internet: Some Ethical and Practical Considerations." In *Between the Cracks of History: Essays on Teaching and Illustrating Folklore*, ed. Francis Edward Abernathy and Carolyn Fiedler, 42–53. Publications of the Texas Folklore Society 55. Nacogdoches, TX: Texas Folklore Society.

Shea, Virginia. 1994. *Netiquette*. San Francisco: Albian.

Sherman, Sharon R. 1998. *Documenting Ourselves: Film, Video, and Culture*. Lexington: University Press of Kentucky.

Shifman, Limor. 2007. "Humor in the Age of Digital Reproduction: Continuity and Change in Internet-Based Comic Texts." *International Journal of Communication* 1: 187–209.

Shirky, Clay. 2008. *Here Comes Everybody: The Power of Organizing Without Organizations*. New York: Penguin Books.

Silver, David, Adrienne Massanari, and Steve Jones, eds. 2006. *Critical Cyberculture Studies*. New York: New York University Press.

Sproull, Lee, and Sara Kiesler. 1992. *Connections: New Ways of Working in the Networked World*. Cambridge, MA: MIT Press.

Stross, Brian. 1999. "The Hybrid Metaphor: From Biology to Culture." *Journal of American Folklore* 112, no. 445: 254–67.

Thompson, Tok. 2011. "Beat-boxing, Mashups, and Cyborg Identity: Folk Music for the 21st Century." *Western Folklore* 70, no. 2: 171–93.

Turkle, Sherry. 2011. *Alone Together: Why We Expect More from Technology and Less from Each Other*. New York: Basic Books.

Underberg, Natalie. 2006. "Virtual and Reciprocal Ethnography on the Internet: The East Mims Oral History Project Website." *Journal of American Folklore* 119 (473): 301–11. http://dx.doi.org/10.1353/jaf.2006.0037.

Weber, Sandra, and Shanly Dixon, eds. 2007. *Growing Up Online: Young People and Digital Technologies*. New York: Palgrave Macmillan. http://dx.doi.org/10.1057/9780230607019.

Westerman, William. 2009. "Epistemology, the Sociology of Knowledge, and the *Wikipedia* Userbox Controversy." In *Folklore and the Internet: Vernacular Expression in a Digital World*, ed. Trevor J. Blank, 123–58. Logan: Utah State University Press.

Wojcik, Daniel. 1997. *The End of the World As We Know It: Faith, Fatalism, and Apocalypse in America*. New York: New York University Press.

Wood, Andrew F., and Matthew J. Smith. 2005. *Online Communication: Linking Technology, Identity, and Culture*. Mahwah, NJ: Lawrence Erlbaum.

About the Author

TREVOR J. BLANK is assistant professor of communication at the State University of New York at Potsdam. He is the editor of *Folklore and the Internet: Vernacular Expression in a Digital World* (Utah State University Press 2009) and *Folk Culture in the Digital Age: The Emergent Dynamics of Human Interaction* (Utah State University Press 2012), co-editor (with Robert Glenn Howard) of *Tradition in the Twenty-First Century: Locating the Role of the Past in the Present* (Utah State University Press 2013), and author of *The Last Laugh: Folk Humor, Celebrity Culture, and Mass-Mediated Disasters in the Digital Age* (University of Wisconsin Press 2013). Currently, he serves as editor to the open-access journal *New Directions in Folklore* (http://scholarworks.iu.edu/journals/index.php/ndif/). Follow him on Twitter @trevorjblank.

Folklore and the Internet is a pioneering examination of the folkloric qualities of the World Wide Web, e-mail, and related digital media. It shows that folk culture, sustained by a new and evolving vernacular, has been a key, since the Internet's beginnings, to language, practice, and interaction online. Users of many sorts continue to develop the Internet as a significant medium for generating, transmitting, documenting, and preserving folklore.

Current Arguments in Folklore

Utah State University Press's Current Arguments in Folklore is a series of short-form publications of provocative original material and selections from foundational titles by leading thinkers in the field. Perfect for the folklore classroom as well as the professional collection, this series provides access to important introductory content as well as innovative new work intended to stimulate scholarly conversation. Volumes are available in paperback or ebook form.